"Now the birth of Jesus Christ was mother Mary was espoused to Joseph, together, she was found with child of the Holy Sprit."

Matthew 1:18

Merry Christmas

Photo Source: CANVA Pro

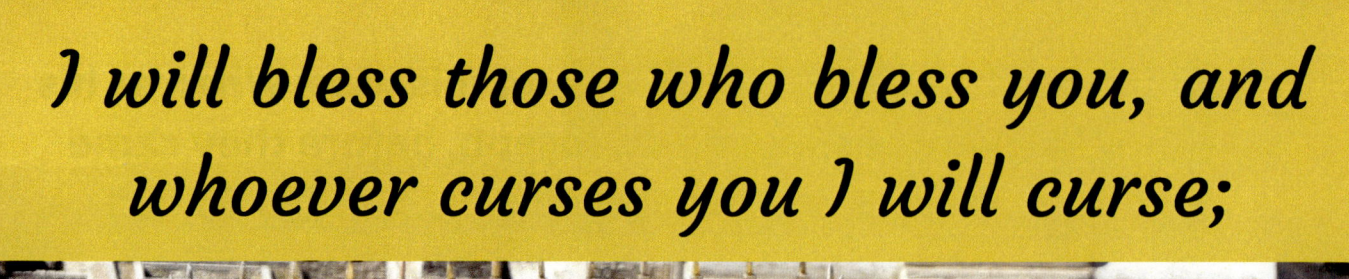

I will bless those who bless you, and whoever curses you I will curse;

Genesis 12:3

"Let your light so shine before men, that they may see your good works, and glorify your Father which is in heaven."

Matthew 5:16 (KJV)

ISSN 2639-7714 (PRINT)
ISSN: 2639-7730 (ONLINE)

Charles Lingerfelt
Editor In Chief

Associate Editor
Vicki VanWey McGill

Editorial Assistant
Carolyn Lingerfelt

Publisher
Christian Times Magazine &
North Texas Freedom Rally

Graphic & Interior Design
Saba A. Anwar & Anil Anwar

Front Cover Photo
Ownership by: North Texas Freedom Rally

CHRISTIAN TIMES MAGAZINE
ISSUE 90 | DECEMBER 2024

Published & Printed in the United States of America

Christian Times Magazine is underwritten by NORTH TEXAS FREEDOM RALLY with Headquarters in Dallas, Texas USA

Copyright © 2024 by Christian Times Magazine

Note: Our content is available for free

charleslingerfelt@ctimesmag.com
www.ctimesmag.com

HELP US CONTINUE SPREADING THE GOOD NEWS –
SUPPORT CHRISTIAN TIMES MAGAZINE!

Warm greetings to you! We hope this letter finds you in good health and high spirits. We are reaching out to you today on behalf of Christian Times Magazine, a publication dedicated to spreading the timeless message of faith, hope, and love. For six years, Christian Times Magazine has been a trusted source of inspiration, encouragement, and biblical insights for thousands of readers like yourself. We believe that by sharing the uplifting stories of fellow believers, discussing relevant issues from a Christian perspective, and providing thoughtful reflections on the Scriptures, we can make a positive impact on the lives of our readers. However, as an independent publication, we face numerous challenges in sustaining our mission and ensuring the continued delivery of high-quality content. Today, we humbly ask for your support to help us keep the Christian Times Magazine thriving and reaching even more individuals with the life-transforming message of the Gospel.

Your donation, no matter the size, will make a significant difference. Here's how your contribution can help:

Printing and Distribution Costs: The funds we receive will go towards covering the expenses associated with printing and distributing each issue of Christian Times Magazine to our subscribers. Your support will ensure that the physical magazine reaches the hands of those who may not have access to online resources.

Editorial Excellence: Your generous donations will enable us to maintain a team of talented writers, editors, and proofreaders who work diligently to produce well-researched, thought-provoking, and spiritually enriching content. With your support, we can continue investing in the editorial process and ensure that every article reflects the highest standards of quality.

Digital Outreach and Engagement: In today's digital age, we recognize the importance of reaching out to a wider audience online. Your contributions will enable us to improve our website, develop engaging multimedia content, and leverage social media platforms to connect with individuals searching for spiritual guidance and Christian perspectives.

We understand that there are countless organizations and causes seeking your support. However, by choosing to contribute to Christian Times Magazine, you are investing in a publication that is dedicated to sharing the timeless truths of the Christian faith and supporting individuals in their spiritual journey. To make a donation, send your contribution by mail to our attached P. O. Box. In addition to our heartfelt gratitude, as a token of our appreciation, we will include your name in our list of valued supporters in an upcoming issue of Christian Times Magazine. Your generosity will be recognized and acknowledged by our readership community. If financial support is not feasible at the moment, we kindly ask for your prayers. Your intercession is invaluable and will strengthen our team, guide our editorial decisions, and enable us to fulfill our mission more effectively.

Thank you for taking the time to read this letter, and for considering supporting Christian Times Magazine. Together, we can continue spreading the good news, providing hope, and inspiring lives through the power of Christian journalism.

May God bless you abundantly for your kindness and generosity.

In Christ's service,

Charles Lingerfeltt
Editor -In-Chief

Send your Donations at

CHRISTIAN TIMES MAGAZINE
P. O. Box 360722
Dallas, TX 75336 USA

OUR MISSION AND PURPOSE:

OUR INTENT AND PURPOSE FOR BEING HERE IS TO PRESENT THE GOSPEL OF THE LORD JESUS CHRIST THROUGH THIS MEDIUM AROUND THE WORLD. OUR GOAL IS TO REACH AS MANY PEOPLE AND NATIONS AS POSSIBLE WITH THIS "GOOD NEWS."

AS CHRISTIANS, WE ARE NEVER ASHAMED TO REACH INTO CULTURES, POLITICAL PERSUASIONS AND NATIONS IN THE SHARING OF THIS GOSPEL MESSAGE. WE ABSOLUTELY BELIEVE THAT WE ARE PLACED HERE ON THE EARTH IN THIS POSITION TO HAVE AN EFFECT UPON TODAY'S SOCIETY. AND WE WILL NEVER BE ASHAMED OF THIS GREAT MESSAGE AND PURPOSE.

THE EDITOR AND PUBLISHER

Charles Lingerfelt

CTM & North Texas Freedom Rally

EDITOR'S NOTE

My End-of-the-Year Message for You!

By Charles Lingerfelt, Editor
CTM Magazine

I like what Robert Lewis says in his book, 'Raising a Modern Day Knight:' "We need men that reject passivity, accept responsibility, lead courageously and expect the greater reward."

The unfortunate truth is that when men fail, society suffers. Men are struggling to find themselves, their place and purpose in society today.

So let me be very frank and honest with you - it matters to God that we have godly men in our society today. It matters even more to God that we have Godly Men in the Church today!

This is my 'Call to action' at this particular time of the year. This year is coming to a close, and another one is about to begin for us in just a few days.

And if anything is most Important in this world today, it is that we need to help Man find their place in life and succeed in the call of God that is upon them.

I want to tell you that you can successfully overcome your struggles and profound experiences related to spiritual growth in your life. Sometimes, men have a difficult time relating to their family, their church, and with other men. But God has given us distinct instructions in the Word that will help us to achieve and be strong men in the sight of God.

One such instance for that is found in the Apostle Paul's writings to the Ephesians: "Finally, be strong in the Lord and in His mighty power." (Ephesians 6:10) Paul knew exactly how important it was to be a strong 'man of God' and decisively, while traveling on the road to Damascus, he heard the voice of the Lord speaking to him and he firmly decided to follow the Christ as his Lord and Savior.

Nothing mattered to him more than following and serving the Lord as his Savior. And because of his love for Jesus, God placed a certain amount of trust in Paul and God endued him with power from on high to make him one of the most important first century apostles.

Everywhere Paul went his presence and power from God caused either a revolution, a revival, or a riot.

And so, as it was in the first century church: the New Testament church - It was very important to God to have men all around in various locations - Men who made a difference with their lives; men who mattered to God - men who wanted to be used of the Almighty in such a way that they would bring other men to God.

And that is exactly what happened in the first century; men became aflamed with the spirit of God and took their power with them wherever they went - and God used them mightily to build the church: the church of the Lord Jesus Christ.

I believe it was Charles Wesley in his early days of preaching across the southern states of the United States who once said to churches all across the South, "If you will get on fire for God, people will come out to watch you burn." And there is a great portion of truth in that phrase. People don't want to attend a "dead church;" that kind of church is the church that has no spirit and fire in their midst. The majority of people in America want to attend a church that is filled with God's Holy Spirit. They want to attend a church that is "on the move for God."

People want to attend a church where the mighty power of the word of God is being preached, believed, and put into action. And people today still want to see miracles happening in the church. They still want to see people turning their lives over to God. They still want to see lives being changed by the spirit of God in our services.

And people still want to see the hearts of men, women and children being changed by the glory of God.

It truly matters to God who you are, and what you are in His kingdom.

God does not only want you to be successful in His kingdom; He wants you to be powerful in His kingdom.

God is calling upon all of us in this New Testament church today, to submit ourselves to Him, to humble ourselves to Him, to repent of our sins and turn away from all ungodliness; and then, He will make us powerful in the world today. God uses powerful men to turn nations around.

Because it matters to God that we live strong, amazing lives before Him, and before all others in our society today.

May God touch us, so that we will matter to the rest of the world and make a difference in this world for the glory of God.

Merry Christmas, my friends, and Happy New Year!

I love You in Jesus,

Charles Lingerfelt

Editor-In-Chief
CHRISTIAN TIMES MAGAZINE
P. O. Box 360722
Dallas, TX 75336 USA
CharlesLingerfelt2018@gmail.com
Charleslingerfelt@ctimesmag.com

CHRISTIAN TIMES MAGZINE
CONTENTS
CHRISTIAN TIMES MAGAZINE ISSUE 90

09 — 'TIS THE SEASON TO BE …
BY LESLEY ROSS RATCLIFFE

12 — ARE YOU LISTENING?
BY ROBERT SUMMERS

14 — THE IMPOSSIBLE GIFT
BY VICKI VANWEY MCGILL

17 — A GRATEFUL NATION REJOICES!
BY KEITH GUINTA

22 — ALL I WANT FOR CHRISTMAS IS PEACE
BY KATHERINE DAIGLE

27 — A CHRISTMAS BLESSING
BY DAVID AYERS

30 — AND THEY PRAYED…
BY PASTOR TIMOTHY LAWSON

32 — A SHORT TREATISE ON THE SIGNIFICANCE OF THE APOCRYPHAL TEXTS: TO SEARCHERS OF TRUTHS
BY ZERNALYN PALMARES

35 — A REVOLUTIONARY ELECTION
BY CAROL MILDER

37 — THE TRUE MEANING OF CHRISTMAS
BY CHARLES LINGERFELT

'TIS THE SEASON TO BE ....

By Lesley Ross Ratcliffe

'Tis the season to be stressed, anxious, hurried, and generally NUTS! For most of us, the holidays bring the busyness of preparing for all the gatherings and gifting. We worry about what to get this friend or that relative. Will they like it, or will they return it? How much should I spend on my Secret Santa gift? Will I finish my decorating in time to host that Christmas gathering? Get the gifts! Wrap the gifts! Give the gifts! And don't even get me started on the baking!

Whew, I'm exhausted just writing about all this hurried holiday frenzy! Is that really what this season is all about? I mean, is that all there is to this season of giving?

My answer is a resounding NO! It is a season of giving, but it is also a season of expectancy, joyful waiting, anticipation, peace, and love. I absolutely love Advent and Christmastide! I love the tradition and liturgy that comes with this season.

The first Sunday after Thanksgiving begins the season of Advent. During Advent, our tradition is to light a candle in the Advent wreath on the first Sunday of Advent and then light an additional candle on the subsequent Sundays to mark the progression of the four weeks of Advent as we anticipate the birth of our Savior, Jesus Christ. Celebrating the season in this way helps to remind me to slow down and focus my heart on the reason for the season.

Our tradition uses an Advent wreath consisting of three purple candles, one pink, and a large white candle in the center of the wreath.

The four candles of the Advent wreath specifically symbolize the Christian concepts of hope (purple), peace (purple), joy (purple) and love (pink), with the fifth candle (white) known as the "Christ candle," symbolizing the arrival of Christmastide.

The Christ candle is lit on Christmas Day, which is the beginning of Christmastide, and can be lit throughout the remainder of the Christmas season into Epiphany. Epiphany is the celebration of Christ's manifestation to the Gentiles, and the Christ candle is white because this is the traditional festal color in the Western Church.

The First Sunday of Advent

The candle of hope reminds us that we are a people of hope and that our hope has come in the form of a promise fulfilled.

From deep in the past, Jeremiah calls to us, "The days are surely coming, says the LORD, when I will fulfill the promise I made to the house of Israel and the house of Judah" (Jeremiah 33:14). Beloved, the days are surely coming when the yearning of the land; the longing of the sun, moon, and stars; the desperate need of the people of earth for flourishing and peace will receive their fulfillment.

While fear, anxiety, misinformation, and suspicion surround us on every side, we choose to watch and wait in hope, preparing our hearts to notice and cooperate with God's grace already at work in our midst. We light this candle of hope as a sign of our commitment to pay attention and prepare for the days that are surely coming and are already here—the days when God's kingdom of love, justice, and mercy will reign.

The Second Sunday of Advent

The candle of peace reminds us not only that we await the arrival of the Prince of Peace, but that we find our peace in our Heavenly Father. He gives a peace that the world cannot take away. It also reminds us that we are called to pursue peace and share the Giver of our peace with our neighbors.

"The prophet Malachi calls us to watch for the messenger God will send us, a messenger who burns with a passion for God's coming salvation. "For he is like a refiner's fire and like fullers' soap; he will sit as a refiner and purifier of silver, and he will purify the descendants of Levi and refine them like gold and silver, until they present offerings to the LORD in righteousness" (Malachi 3:2b-3).

In a world driven by a passion to maintain the status quo, we choose to live with a passion for God's peace, to listen to those who call us to righteousness, and to submit ourselves to God's grace, that we might be refined and purified until we reflect God's love throughout the earth.

We light this candle of peace as a sign of our commitment to passionately pursue the work of making peace in our hearts, our families, our communities, and throughout the earth until God's kingdom comes on earth as it is in heaven.

The Third Sunday of Advent

The candle of joy is lit to remind us of the joy of the Lord and the joy His birth brought to a weary world. It is that joy which we should carry throughout the year.

No matter what troubles overwhelm us today, Isaiah reminds us that in all of our preparation and passionate pursuit of God's coming kingdom, we must not forget that God's salvation has come and is coming. "With joy you will draw water from the wells of salvation" (Isaiah 12:3). With joy you will remember that God's salvation is already present among us.

Faced with the troubles and the suffering of the world, we choose to live in joyful presence to God and one another. We will not turn away from the pain and the hurt in our world, and we will not stop rejoicing in God, whose salvation fills us to overflowing that God's love might flow through us and flood our troubled world with hope, peace, and joy.

We light this candle of joy as a sign of our commitment to be present to ourselves, our friends, our families, and our neighbors that in sharing our vulnerable lives we might share in the glorious joy of God's salvation.

The Fourth Sunday of Advent

We light the candle of love to remind us that God loved us so much that He sent His Only Son to be born in a humble manger in a stinky ol' barn. As we light this candle, we renew our commitment to love others as Christ loves us.

When the people were looking for deliverance, the prophet Micah declared, "But you, O Bethlehem of Ephrath … from you shall come forth for me one who is to rule in Israel, whose origin is from of old, from ancient day"' (Micah 5:2).

But what if Micah is also talking to us, proclaiming, "But you, O (insert your name), from you shall come forth for me…." What? What might God be calling forth from us?

God invites us to receive the promise of God's salvation and the sustenance of God's mercy and grace, enabling us to live the promise as God-bearers to the world. As Christ was born in Bethlehem, so too we answer God's invitation to have Christ born among us today and every day.

We light this candle of love as a sign of our commitment to live as people of God's promise, a promise of salvation and flourishing for all people that springs forth from God's love for all creation.

I pray that in this season of hustle and bustle we will take a moment to stop and breathe. Breathe in the hope, peace, joy, and love that the Christ Child brings. In this season of giving, I pray that we will all be mindful of the greatest gift ever given and give thanks to the Prince of Peace. The heavens are full of His glory, and the angels shout, "Glory to God in the highest, and on earth peace, goodwill to men" (Luke 2:14, NKJV). May the Christ of Christmas be alive in our hearts and actions all year long.

Merry Christmas!

(The narratives in italics are taken from The United Methodist Church Book of Discipline, 2024.)

ARE YOU LISTENING?

By Robert Summers

"…because the time is near." Revelation 1:3

"And behold, there was a man in Jerusalem whose name was Simeon; and the same man was just and devout, waiting for the consolation of Israel; and the Holy Ghost was upon him. And it had been revealed to him by the Holy Spirit that he would not see death before he had seen the Lord's Christ." Luke 2: 25-26 NKJV

Simeon, the devout old servant of the Lord heard a specific word from the Holy Spirit directing him to the temple the same day Mary and Joseph brought Baby Jesus to be dedicated on His eighth day. Simeon's name is a derivative of the Hebrew word shema. The name means "he who hears" or "the listener." Luke did not call him a priest. The priests in that day ministered under the Sadducees. They were unlikely to be spirit led. We do know Simeon was a prophet. His prophecy is recorded in Luke as a true prophetic word. All true prophets are, like Simeon, listeners.

Today everyone has a megaphone with which to speak (call that a cellphone). There are many words from many, many voices. Who are you listening to? Today?

Are you spending more time on the internet than you do to prayerfully listen to the voice of God? God is always speaking. He has so much more of the beauty and goodness of Christ Jesus to reveal. As the Hebrews epistle says, "Concerning him we have much to say, and it is hard to explain since you have become dull of hearing and disinclined to listen." (Hebrews 5:11). Our very faith depends upon our listening. *So then faith comes by hearing, and hearing by the Word of God.* (Romans 10:17) Ask the Holy Spirit to help you hear.

Be careful to hear. But be careful also what you hear. There are many voices in the air that have no reluctance to deceive, to introduce themselves as the "Holy Ghost!" Every listener needs discernment.

. Every listener needs to be willing to test all things. Paul charges us in I Thessalonians 5:21, "Test all things, hold fast what is good." We test words of prophecy, not to discourage the gift, but rather to hold on to the valid word as a good and proven word.

In this age, this end time season we are in, we must be listening like our life depends upon it. Destruction comes suddenly! Storms can blow down on us as soon as we get as out into the middle of the lake. All we really want is a happy

little cruise to the other side. A storm comes suddenly. Out of fear we cry "Master, we are perishing!" Here is the lesson, so listen up!

Had we listened and had we caught the word of Jesus, "Let us cross over to the other side of lake" (Luke 8:22) we would know that we had His word and that we would make it across. Remember, every lake has another side. We will make it across and through the storm to the other side. Jesus said so. His word never fails. But are we listening? Are we really hearing? Faith comes by hearing. So let us all become listeners like dear old Simeon. Who knows what kind of glorious encounter we may have. Who knows?

No eye has seen,
No ear has heard,
No mind has conceived
What God has prepared
For those who love Him.

(Paul in I Corinthians 2:9 quotes from Isaiah 64:4)

THE IMPOSSIBLE GIFT

By Vicki VanWey McGill

I often share my heart when writing for you, precious Christian Times Reader. It is when we share our hearts that we make connections with others who are celebrating, or searching, or struggling, or giving up in life. It is when we share our hearts that we are able to discover together the deepest things of life, especially the things that reveal God's working in our lives. As Christmas approaches this year, my heart urgently begs to be heard by those who will, by God's intervention, happen upon this magazine at this time and upon this article this very moment.

For those who are grieving, or are fearful, or are hungry to understand the meaning of life, it seems that this Christmas should be the time of relief, or comfort, or the dawning of new understandings that will carry us through this life. Often the answers come when we put down our swords, our maps, our objects of affection, and just listen with our whole being. When we give up our own solutions and quietly submit to God, often our answers come.

When Mary, mother of Jesus, was told by the angel Gabriel that she would give birth to a son, she found it too incredible, according to man's comprehension, since she was still a virgin. However, though she did not understand how God was going to perform this miracle of a virgin birth, Mary submitted wholly to God to become and to do those things planned for her- and for her first born son, Jesus- since before the foundation of the world was laid. Mary was willing to accept this impossible gift.

The story of Christ's birth is a widely known history. It is history because these things actually happened. It is documented in the most reliable and time tested writings the world has ever tried to disprove- The Bible. Luke chapter 2 is a good place to find part of the story if you are not familiar with this account of the first arrival of the Jewish Messiah. The themes of Christmas continue to repeat the original threads of angels, shepherds, a manger bed in a lowly stall, a bright and shining star that eventually led wise men from the east to behold this infant king. Some people of the world- then and now- find it difficult to believe this beautiful record of how the Savior of all mankind was delivered by a simple handmaiden. The people of the world realize that a savior, born to a virgin human, is the impossible- and unlikely- gift. Yet, those who open their hearts and their minds and those who are willing to step away from all the clamor and naysayers, can find the Savior of their lives as thousands have done through the centuries.

If Jesus is who the Bible says he is, why don't we have some tomb to go visit that points to a decaying buried body? Why do we have to search for him with something so elusive as a heart's desire to draw close to the truth and the Creator of all things? Why is there, instead of an ancient body in an ancient grave, just an empty tomb and no body to be found? It is because the impossible gift was given over two thousand years ago. Jesus, willing to walk the earth for 33 years, and willing to submit to death on a cross, and willing to become the sacrifice that has the power to wipe away the sins of every person, was willing to fulfill the Father's plan and to become the Impossible Gift. Jesus, who was crucified, dead, and buried, was resurrected. For those of us who have found this Impossible Gift did so by accepting that Jesus was born of a virgin, walked the earth healing and performing miracles, was unjustly nailed to a cross, suffered the death of a criminal yet never committed even one offense, and came back to life in order to offer eternal life to every man, woman, and child. Those who accept Him, have accepted his promise of complete forgiveness of all sins, and are recipients of The Impossible Gift.

During this season of Christmas, will you surrender your incredulous thinking? Will you simply bow before him in your heart, and humbly accept the offer of eternal life? Will you accept this Impossible Gift?

****

If you have access to any device that can deliver information as well as music, find time to listen to the Christmas carol, "The Carol of the Bells". It is a beautifully haunting song that echoes the joy intended for us to experience during this season of the year.

Carol of the Bells

Ding dong ding dong ding
Ding dong ding dong ding
Ding dong ding dong ding
Ding dong ding dong ding
Hark how the bells
Sweet silver bells
All seem to say
Throw cares away
Christmas is here
Bringing good cheer
To young and old
Meek and the bold
Ding, dong, ding, dong
That is their song
With joyful ring
All caroling
One seems to hear
Words of good cheer
From ev'rywhere
Filling the air
Ding dong ding dong ding
Oh how they pound
Raising the sound
O'er hill and dale
Telling their tale
Gaily they ring
While people sing
Songs of good cheer
Christmas is here
Merry, merry, merry, merry Christmas
Merry, merry, merry, merry Christmas

Hark how the bell
Sweet silver bells
All seem to say
Throw cares away
Christmas is here
Bringing good cheer
To young and old
Meek and the bold
Ding, dong, ding, dong
That is their song
With joyful ring
All caroling
One seems to hear
Words of good cheer
From ev'rywhere
Filling the air
Merry, merry, merry, merry Christmas
Merry, merry, merry, merry Christmas
On on they send
On without end
Their joyful tone to every home
Ding dong ding dong ding
Ding dong ding dong ding
Christmas is here
Bringing good cheer
To young and old
Meek and the bold
Ding dong ding dong ding
That is their song
With joyful ring
Ding dong ding dong ding

written by Grant Geissman
lyrics © Liffey Publishing Ltd., Jrm Music, Video Helper

Christian Times Magazine – www.ctimesmag.com   PAGE 17

A GRATEFUL NATION REJOICES!

By Keith Guinta

www.winepatch.org

This article was originally published at Intercessors For America, used by permission of the author.

Photo: George Whitefield, Preaching in the Colonies.

November 12, 2024

Breaking: The Lord has declared victory and a grateful nation rejoices!

The November 2020 election results rightly left countless millions distraught and filled with dread for the future of our country. Out of that concern and lament, a national prayer movement launched, which possibly would not have formed otherwise. Four long years of faithful, fervent, and travailing prayer brought us these miraculous election results of 2024. When the Lord hears the prayers of a nation, it is fitting to thank Him with the same zeal we beseeched Him with.
"He answered their prayers because they trusted Him." ~ I Chronicles 5:20

To those who knelt low on their kneelers and those who were seated high atop the watchman's wall, give thanks to the Lord with a grateful heart! To those who were hungry for the meat of brave preachers and those who were thirsty for the words of the prophets, give thanks to the Lord with a grateful heart! To those who spoke the truth in the face of lies and those who employed the gift of distinguishing between spirits, give thanks to the Lord with a grateful heart!

To those who resisted the leaven of Herod and those who released the leaven of the Kingdom, give thanks to the Lord with a grateful heart! To those who prayed without food and those who worshiped without ceasing, give thanks to the Lord with a grateful heart! To those who suffered loss for their beliefs and those who were reviled, and persecuted, and had all kinds of evil uttered against them: Rejoice! For great is your reward in heaven.

I never set out to be a political commentator, and in the familiar sense of the term, I am still not one. I am a brother of Christ who is deeply disturbed to see both believers and churches succumb to the deceptions of wokeness, leftism, and globalism. The antichrist spirit has enthroned itself on this rotted, three-legged stool, the same stool from which winsome preachers muse on the nuance of abortion, the horrors of whiteness, and the unforgivable sins of America's founding.

These are often the very same leaders who scold Christians not to be political.

The word politics is immediately construed as the corrupt and conniving tactics of crooked, public self-servants. But in its etymological sense, politics, from polis, is simply the spiritual or secular governance of a citizenry and its behavior. This is precisely why the New Testament church in the First Century was not called a synagogue or a temple but the Ecclesia. In Roman times, the Ecclesia was an authoritative gathering or council of the polis and was actively embedded in the center of the public square.

Witnessing how many preachers remained silent about the recent election has been both dismaying and disheartening. While I have written much on our presidency this year, I wrote one final plea last week charging pastors to equip their sheep before they stepped into the shearing booth. Tragically, even on the Sunday before the election, many pastors chose to remain silent.

"It is a poor sermon that gives no offense; that neither makes the hearer displeased with himself nor with the preacher." ~ George Whitefield

What Kind of Blue Did He Say?

A recently published national map exhibits the ten most post-Christian cities in America. Two of these cities are on the West Coast, and the remaining eight are here in the Northeast. You don't have to be painter Bob Ross to quickly see this glaringly obvious portrait — The Northeast paints its political palette not with Van Dyke Brown, Titanium White, or even Bright Red. No, the once sacred cradle of two Great Awakenings prefers its politics in deep Phthalo Blue.

This happy-little axiomatic equation is obvious: Deep blue politics yields post-Christian culture, and post-Christian culture breeds deep blue politics. So, to all the church leaders and pulpiteers intent on "bringing the gospel" to New England, you must break through the fourth wall and understand that you are more than gatherers, evangelists, and encouragers—you are thought-shapers.

The apostle Paul teaches that those who have received the Holy Spirit can know the thoughts of God. Conversely, unspiritual believers cannot understand God's thoughts and even deem them to be foolish. (I Corinthians 2) Imagine, there are myriads of saints marching through the pearly gates right now who unfortunately missed out on how the mind of Christ operates within the Kingdom of God here on earth.

A believer may possess a biblical worldview, but if they lack a Kingdom way of thinking, they may not robustly release the salt, light, and leaven of the Kingdom into the public square. By choosing to remain silent throughout the election season and thereby not helping the saints grow in Kingdom thinking, our pastors became political in the worst sense of the word.

"Rejoice with those who rejoice, and mourn with those who mourn." ~ Romans 12:15

Because some pastors carefully calculated their pre-election silence, they have relegated themselves to extending their self-imposed muzzling into the post-election season. The church leaders who viewed their campuses as potential war zones and refused to risk diminishing the size of their ranks are now unable to provide the lambs with the pastoral care they require.

Using broad estimation, imagine that half of your congregation was fervently praying, fasting, and interceding on behalf of our nation these past four years. These warriors experienced an ongoing threat of peril right up until Pennsylvania was called, at which point these spirit-filled patriots began rejoicing with gratefulness and jubilee.

These faithful and grateful rejoicers walked into church the Sunday after the election with a deepened desire to worship the Lord and celebrate His favor and goodness. It was a victory for them, and they knew that a great evil had been thwarted in the unseen realms. It was time for the church to rejoice!

Alas, because their pastor chose to refrain from equipping these intercessors, he disqualified himself from rejoicing with them. As far as anyone could tell as they entered the Sabbath biosphere, nothing of import transpired that week, so it was Sunday business as usual.

Rejoice with those who are rejoicing.

Likewise, consider that the other half of your congregation was deeply conditioned by the media, news outlets, and the current administration and genuinely believed this election would place our nation under despotic, authoritarian control. For them, a great wave of dread was released when Pennsylvania was called, at which point these believers began weeping with fear and great anger.

These shaken and unsettled mourners walked into church the Sunday after the election with an admixture of woe and fear, wondering how God could allow this. For them, it was a cataclysmic defeat and they believed a great force of good was vanquished by evil. It was time for the church to mourn. Alas, because their pastor chose to refrain from properly preparing this group of people, he disqualified himself from addressing their mourning. As far as anyone could tell as they entered the Sabbath biosphere, nothing of import transpired that week, so it was Sunday business as usual. Mourn with those who are mourning.

The impact of our preaching is not intended solely for the sound systems within the biosphere and the hidden chambers of people's hearts. The effects of robust preaching shape thought, invoke action, and should be visible in the public square.

America's Next Chance to Please The Lord:

The thunderous preachers of the Great Awakening, like Whitefield and Edwards, not only shaped the thoughts and ideas upon which our nation was founded but they were also kicked out of their pious biospheres. Jonathan Edwards was fired from his church in North Hampton, MA, over the issue of Communion, and George Whitefield was booted for boldly speaking against the establishment churches.

What their opponents meant for evil, God used for good. These ousted orators became far more effective as open-air preachers, no longer sprinkling the saturated in the pews but feeding the famished in the fields of New England.

The preaching of Whitefield profoundly forged Benjamin Franklin's thinking, and he often remarked on the fruit evident in the streets. Franklin wrote of Whitefield's preaching in his autobiography:

"It was wonderful to see the change soon made in the manners of our inhabitants. From being thoughtless or indifferent about religion, it seems as if all the world were growing religious, so that one could not walk thro' the town in an evening without hearing psalms sung in different families of every street."

~

The Autobiography of Benjamin Franklin, p. 146

For me, election night was profoundly humbling. I have listened, discerned, and thought carefully about politics, culture, and the Kingdom these past few years and have paid a personal price for doing so. But when Pennsylvania was called, I was overcome by a weighty sense of history. While there will potentially be tens or hundreds or thousands of future elections, the election of 2024 may turn out to be the most consequential of my lifetime and I am humbled to know that my analysis, thoughts, and convictions are digitally stored for lifetimes to come.

Early on, I deflected attention from the man and urged readers to focus on policy. But then we watched this man, Donald Trump, endure an unending onslaught of false accusations, the Steele Dossier, the Russia Collusion, two impeachments, punitive lawsuits designed to bankrupt and imprison him, and the entire regime machinery run 24/7 smear campaigns, forced every American to lean in and look closer.

But when that bullet ripped through his ear just millimeters from taking his head off, it was no longer about policy. When he rose off the platform, clenched his fist, and yelled, "Fight! Fight! Fight! it was all about the man.

Yes, it is a time of rejoicing. And, I bear enough insight to understand why so many are mourning. But right now, this is very humbling. The Lord has given America another chance we may not have deserved, and I pray we can live up to the immensity of His grace extended to us.

"'Let everyone call urgently on God. Let them give up their evil ways and their violence. Who knows? God may yet relent and with compassion turn from His fierce anger so that we will not perish.' When God saw what they did and how they turned from their evil ways, He relented and did not bring on them the destruction He had threatened." ~
The King of Nineveh in the Book of Jonah 3:8-10

The impact of our preaching is not intended solely for the sound systems within the biosphere and the hidden chambers of people's hearts. The effects of robust preaching shape thought, invoke action, and should be visible in the public square.

America's Next Chance to Please The Lord:

The thunderous preachers of the Great Awakening, like Whitefield and Edwards, not only shaped the thoughts and ideas upon which our nation was founded but they were also kicked out of their pious biospheres. Jonathan Edwards was fired from his church in North Hampton, MA, over the issue of Communion, and George Whitefield was booted for boldly speaking against the establishment churches.

What their opponents meant for evil, God used for good. These ousted orators became far more effective as open-air preachers, no longer sprinkling the saturated in the pews but feeding the famished in the fields of New England.

The preaching of Whitefield profoundly forged Benjamin Franklin's thinking, and he often remarked on the fruit evident in the streets. Franklin wrote of Whitefield's preaching in his autobiography:

"It was wonderful to see the change soon made in the manners of our inhabitants. From being thoughtless or indifferent about religion, it seems as if all the world were growing religious, so that one could not walk thro' the town in an evening without hearing psalms sung in different families of every street."

The Autobiography of Benjamin Franklin, p. 146

Keith Guinta is, In Reverse Order: Mountaineer, Standup Comic, Ironman, Marathoner, Coach, Church Planter, Small Business Owner, Coffee Roaster, Rookie Blogger, Worship Leader, Father, Husband, Younger Brother of Christ. He is the inspiring force and voice behind his blog and website, The Wine Patch. You are encouraged to be uplifted by visiting and subscribing on his website for a host of Christian based blogs which look at today's world of politics, culture, and personal spirituality at

https://www.winepatch.org

ALL I WANT FOR CHRISTMAS IS PEACE

By Katherine Daigle

Photo Provided by Katherine Daigle

As we approach the Christmas season, the traditional feeling of joy and optimism that fills the air finally has a strong and realistic background for our nation and the world. The lights are shining, the carols are playing, and there's a renewed hope that the coming year will bring us closer to the peace and unity we have prayed for. For many of us, this season carries a deeper meaning—one that celebrates the birth of Christ and the promise of peace that He brings to our hearts and our world. There is also one more reason to celebrate: President Donald Trump's re-election, a victory that we, as a united community of faith-based conservatives, have fervently prayed for.

A Victory Guided by God's Hand

For tens of millions of Americans, President Trump's victory as the 47th President of the United States isn't just a political win—it's a divine affirmation, a validation of our shared faith and beliefs. It's a clear sign that God's hand guides our nation and world toward peace, strength, and restoration, using him as an instrument of change. Trump's return to the Oval Office is the return of a leader who can steer this country and the world toward peace.

As we reflect on what this victory means, we can't ignore the miraculous timing of it all. God works in mysterious ways, and for those of us who have been praying for peace in our own homes and the homes of our allies, President Trump's victory is a direct and clear answer.

His unwavering view on security, religious freedom, and peace abroad assures us that God is at work, guiding him to be the leader of the free nation – especially now as these evil villains transform their influence and apply their will over our faith and freedoms we need during these uncertain times.

Faith and Divine Purpose of God Our Savior and Trump, his Messenger

The righteous fury and moral outrage of the American people, who have built this country grounded in faith in God, showed at this point that we are at the precipice and that we are ready to stand with Trump and protect our constitutional independence, principles, freedoms, and ideals.

So why is Donald Trump the messenger for the people, a warrior, a soldier with the world's weight on his shoulders? Why has the world reached out in protests and prayer, carrying his words in mantras? Have they had enough? Are we there yet?

Donald Trump represents everything the marginalized patriots and the silent majority of conservatives have been waiting for. He is strong on national security, an experienced former President of the United States, and a successful businessman who understands how capitalism works and how he can use it to revitalize the economy.

Perhaps most importantly, President Trump is not afraid to speak his mind. Countries worldwide respect this man for his word because it is powerful. People trust him after being forced for years to ingest the likes of many incompetent politicians and cowardly, arrogant, selfish deep-state losers, who grudgingly paid them reluctant lip service when they weren't flagrantly embracing liberal Marxist policies and accepted payments in trade for the people's freedoms.

Faithful conservatives, at last, have labored for four years to re-elect our strong conservative President, Donald J. Trump, with his hand-picked MAGAvengers (Punishers) to date who genuinely believe in the same principles. He is not being silent nor diplomatic – about anything. He says what he likes and says and does exactly what he thinks with the hand of God on his shoulder.

Announced

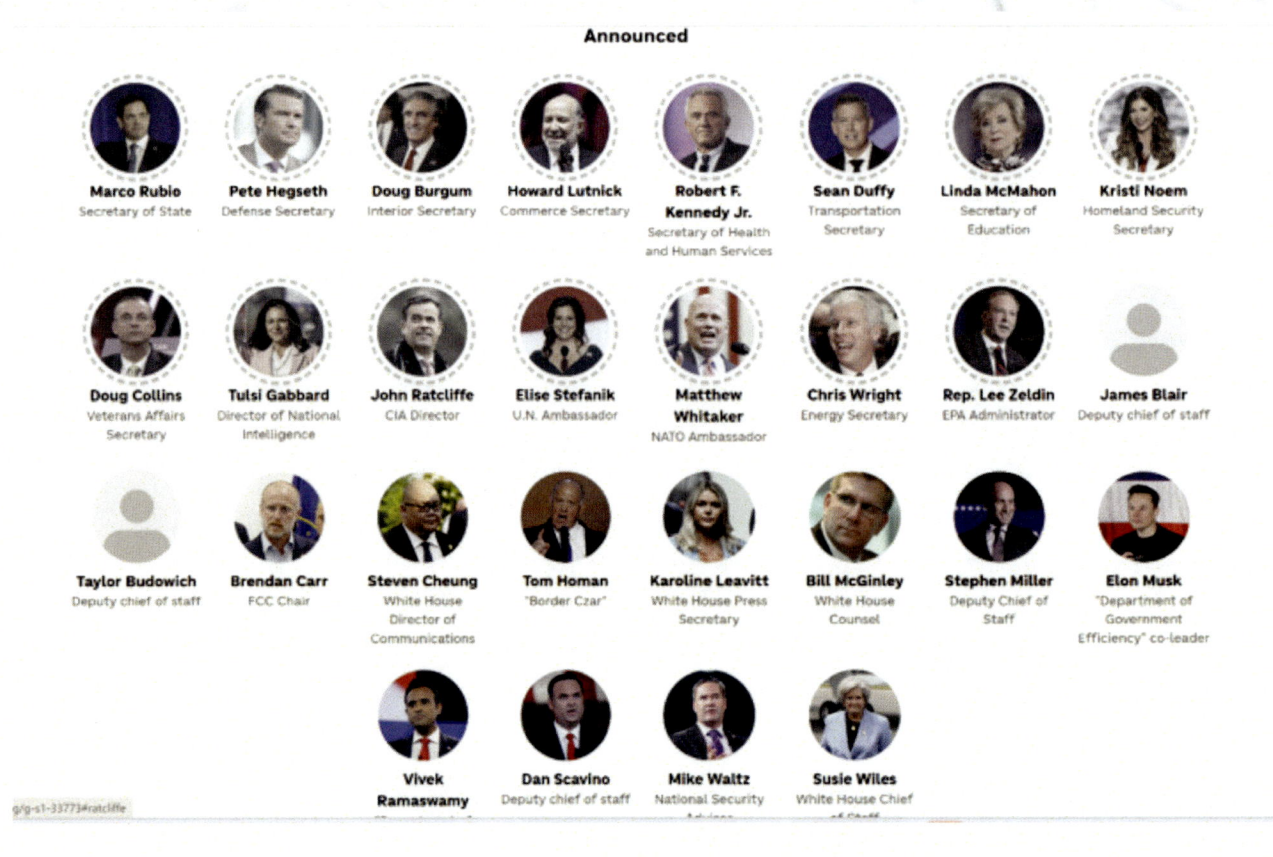

Marco Rubio — Secretary of State	Pete Hegseth — Defense Secretary	Doug Burgum — Interior Secretary	Howard Lutnick — Commerce Secretary
Robert F. Kennedy Jr. — Secretary of Health and Human Services	Sean Duffy — Transportation Secretary	Linda McMahon — Secretary of Education	Kristi Noem — Homeland Security Secretary
Doug Collins — Veterans Affairs Secretary	Tulsi Gabbard — Director of National Intelligence	John Ratcliffe — CIA Director	Elise Stefanik — U.N. Ambassador
Matthew Whitaker — NATO Ambassador	Chris Wright — Energy Secretary	Rep. Lee Zeldin — EPA Administrator	James Blair — Deputy chief of staff
Taylor Budowich — Deputy chief of staff	Brendan Carr — FCC Chair	Steven Cheung — White House Director of Communications	Tom Homan — "Border Czar"
Karoline Leavitt — White House Press Secretary	Bill McGinley — White House Counsel	Stephen Miller — Deputy Chief of Staff	Elon Musk — "Department of Government Efficiency" co-leader
Vivek Ramaswamy	Dan Scavino — Deputy chief of staff	Mike Waltz — National Security Advisor	Susie Wiles — White House Chief of Staff

Faith, Freedom, and Trump: Embodying the Spirit of American Exceptionalism this Christmas

This Christmas season offers a profound opportunity to reflect on the ideals that have shaped America as a beacon of hope, resilience, and freedom. Faith and freedom—two pillars of American exceptionalism—have guided the nation through its most challenging moments. President Donald Trump, through his leadership and vision, has sought to rekindle these ideals, creating a legacy that resonates far beyond politics.

As the Bible reminds us, "For I know the plans I have for you," declares the Lord, "plans to prosper you and not to harm you, plans to give you hope and a future" (Jeremiah 29:11).

Trump's leadership is part of a larger, divine plan that includes protecting America, defending its allies, and the restoration of justice and common sense for all. In a world plagued by globalism, corruption, and threats to our republic, Trump's re-election is a turning point in our world. His return to the presidency is a beacon of hope, a reassurance that our faith and prayers have not been in vain, for those who have long believed that America and its allies were due for a revival of strength, faith, and divine purposefulness.

Christmas is Peace for All

Christmas is, above all, a season of peace.

In Luke 2:14, we read the angels proclaim:
""Glory to God in the highest heaven, and on earth peace to those on whom his favor rests."" ("Luke 2:14 NIV: "Glory to God in the highest heaven, and on earth peace ...")

This verse says that the birth of Jesus Christ brought peace to the world, a peace that we are meant to share.

As we celebrate Christmas, we celebrate peace—not just in our hearts or homes but in our world. This message is especially important in a world torn by division, war, and uncertainty.
One of the most encouraging aspects of President Trump's leadership has been his commitment to peace and ability to deliver.

Throughout his previous presidency, Trump made it clear that he has always been and will continue to focus on putting an end to senseless, pointless global conflicts that hurt both America and its allies. His efforts to broker peace agreements between Israel and several Arab nations were historic, proving that peace is achievable even in regions long known for strife. Now, he is ready to do it again and on a much bigger scale than ever, thanks to the previous administration that has put the world on the verge of a new nuclear crisis. We can all celebrate his promise to bring American troops home, end endless wars, and prioritize peace over conflict.

The Bible tells us:

"Blessed are the peacemakers, for they will be called children of God" (Matthew 5:9).

Even before the official inauguration, the president-elect's actions, words, and nominations have shown that he is a leader who values peace. That is why his victory feels like a step toward peace even before the start of his new presidency.

A Christmas Wish
As we celebrate Christmas this year, our wish may sound simple and inconsequential: peace on Earth. But we pray for a world where nations come together, families are safe, and communities can thrive without the threat of violence or division, knowing that now we have a leader who knows how to make and keep those promises. We still remember that peace begins with each of us. It starts in our hearts, in our homes, and in our communities. But it also requires strong leadership and a commitment from all of us to stand up together for what is right.

And a Hopeful New Year

As we close out this year and look toward the future, let us remember the valid reason for the season. Christ came to bring peace; we are called to be instruments of that peace.

In the words of John 1:29: "Behold, the Lamb of God, who takes away the sin of the world."

Through His sacrifice, we can have peace that surpasses all understanding.

My wish for this Christmas is simple: may we all work together toward a world filled with harmony, where peace is not just a dream but a daily reality. Let's come together and pray for hope in this season of light and remember the importance of compassion, unity, loyalty to our nation, and understanding of faiths across Earth. Merry Christmas to all, and may we step into the new year with a renewed commitment to world peace.

President Trump's re-election reminds us that God is still in control and guiding us toward the peace we so desperately need. May the peace of Christ fill your hearts this Christmas and beyond.

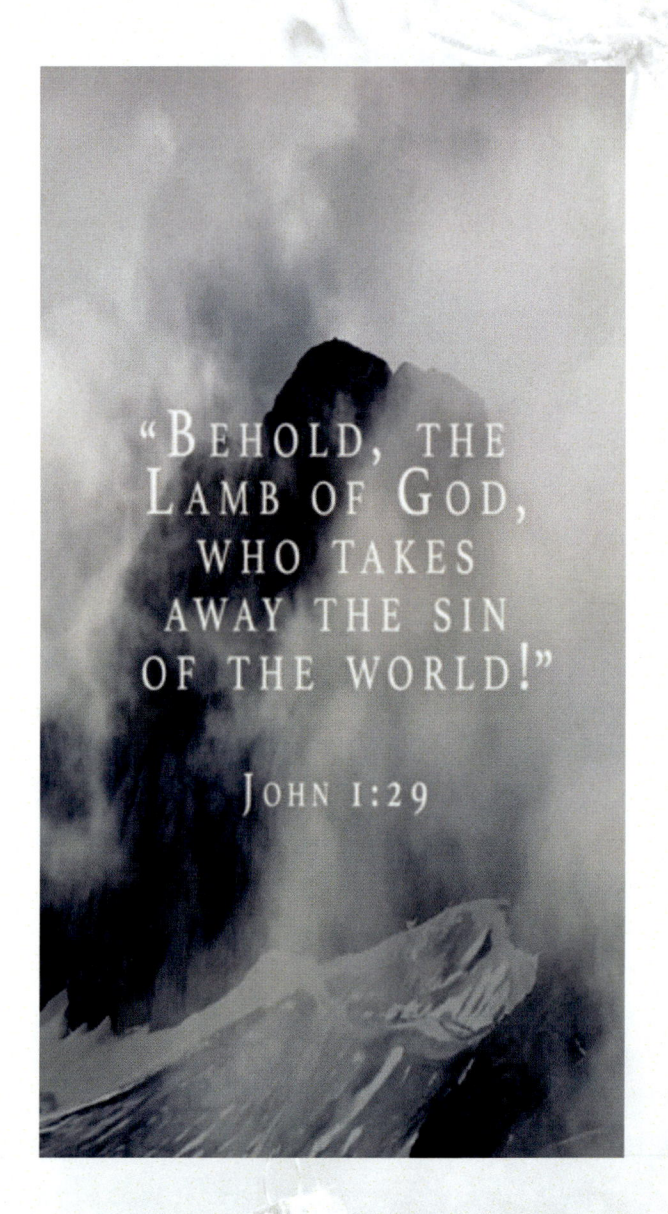

"BEHOLD, THE LAMB OF GOD, WHO TAKES AWAY THE SIN OF THE WORLD!"

JOHN 1:29

A CHRISTMAS BLESSING

By David Ayers

(Tennessee)

As a Christian and certainly from a Christian's perspective the three most important events in human history were the birth, death, and resurrection of the Lord Jesus Christ. Now whether you agree with me or not, we do celebrate the Christmas season based on the events around the birth of the Christ child.

Accounts of this blessed event are given in two different locations in the Gospels of Matthew and Luke in the New Testament.

Now, in this amazing story of a royal deity of a divine Son and his Holy Father in total agreement that he would put aside his deity in heaven with all the blessing of such a wondrous existence and become one of us born as a common man in the most humble of conditions.

What manner of Holy Father and Son would do this except for their true love for all of us?

Maybe best described by KJV in John 3:16, "For God so loved the world, that he gave His only begotten Son, that whosoever believeth in him should not perish, but have everlasting life."

Turning back to the Master's humble entry into this earth, we also want to remember the glorious heavenly events at the same time.

There was no room at the Inn when Mary and Joseph arrived into Bethlehem to pay taxes, so Jesus was 'born in a stable and layed in a manger.'

An angel appeared to three shepherds watching over their flock in the fields to announce the arrival of a New king child.

Three wise men from the East were guided by a star to the location of the Christ child. A more detailed account of this birth and the events that occurred during this time are given in Matthew, Chapters 1 & 2 and Luke, Chapters 1 & 2(KJV). Matthew leans more to The Wise Men story following the star with Luke more from the sheep-shepherds perspective - which also highlighted more of the heavenly celebration.

Christmas plays, out of necessity, condense the events of both Matthew and Luke which is only logical.

Throughout the years, this glorious event has become more about a season of celebration given to the secular/commercial view of Christmas; but this cannot take away from the real significance of what our Lord's birth has meant for the human race.

When you reflect on all the religions of this world, I know of no other one which has claimed divinity and has both sent and sacrificed themselves for the good of mankind. If there is one, please enlighten me. I would really like to know!

It begs the question, "if God considers us that important - Why do we not value Him and His Son more important?" Sadly, we as humans have always neglected to honor our Lord in a way that is truly worthy. To put some heartfelt consideration to this matter, would you go as far as to send your son to live among a fallen people knowing that he would be criticized and ridiculed for the sake of a prideful people who put him to death. Only a God and Son of pure love could fulfill such an undertaking for the redemption of all people everywhere. I suppose if I could live a thousand lifetimes, I would not even begin to pay the debt The Lord Jesus paid for me.

The heavenly celebration must have been something to witness with the special proclamation from Luke 14, "Glory to God in the highest, and on earth peace, good will toward men."

I would not normally use any type of poetry in an article like this, but since it seems to fit with the season and maybe helps highlight a point - I'll insert this one:

"Oh to envision a night so clear
In eager anticipation that a King's entry was near,
Did the stars shine brighter in their places to be,
To accompany a star for the Wise men to see?

The shepherds and angel did seek,
of the Christ child the prophets did speak,
A celebration of heavenly delight
from a great host from heaven that night.

From glory, surely an angelic choir did sing,
If in heaven a bell there did ring
Glory to the newborn king!"

Christian Times Magazine – www.ctimesmag.com

A Christmas Blessing - Keep Christ in Christmas - He is the Christmas Blessing!

Merry Christmas to Everyone!

MERRY Christmas and Happy New Year

And They Prayed...

By Pastor Timothy Lawson
Vision United Worship Center, Bristol Tennessee

During the time of the early church, persecution was not at all uncommon. This is evident all throughout the Book of Acts. These believers in Jesus faced banishment from the temple. They faced arrest and trial before the Jewish High Priest. Some, like Stephen even gave their lives for the cause of Christ. The apostle James was even killed with a sword by King Herod's men.

When this puppet king saw how much the killing of James pleased the leaders of the Jewish temple, he sought to go even further. Herod plotted to arrest the leader of the church and try Peter in his court. Herod began to conduct this hideous plan and arrested Peter and put him in prison intending to bring him to trial after Passover. It can be certain that this trial would end in an execution. I believe that the church in Jerusalem thought so as well. Did they run and hide like other believers had? Did they remain secluded in their homes? Absolutely not! They had church.

These believers banded together and met in the house of John Mark's mother, Mary. They did not gather to form a committee to study the situation. They did not plot a rescue or revenge. The church did the only thing that counted. They prayed.

Those prayers did not go unheard. God dispatched an angel to that prison to set Peter free. Peter was bound by chains and guarded by sixteen of Herod's best soldiers.

This, I believe, is where the church of today has lost something. This is where we have gotten off track. What do I mean by that? Today, our prayer life is weaker than it should be. It is something that many see as something that they must do instead of the place to go to for their source of strength. The first century church was a church that was often united in prayer. Their prayer life was truly a group effort. In Acts chapter 2 verse one, we see a notable example of this, And when the day of Pentecost was fully come, they were all with one accord in one place. The believers were all gathered in the Upper Room for one purpose and one purpose alone.

They were there as Jesus instructed them to be, praying for the promise of the Holy Spirit. There were no personal agendas. There was no gossip or infighting. No one took preeminence. They were there as one people, with one purpose, and God moved and answered their prayer. This was also the case with the church praying for their leader. They prayed with power and with authority. They prayed with purpose and they prayed all in one accord. Today we can't even pray five minutes without being distracted or pulled away.

Growing up in the late sixties and early seventies, I remember most every church had a service with a name that we no longer see. It was Mid-Week Prayer service. Those meetings were powerful. They, I believe, resembled the prayer gatherings that we just described earlier. These prayer meetings brought people together but they also drew people closer to God. What happened? I am not exactly sure, but this is something that we need to get back to. Jesus declared when He cleared the temple that His house was to be a house of prayer.

Imagine what would happen if we indeed took prayer more seriously in our church services. I am not talking about the altar call at the end of our services. I am talking about a service totally and completely dedicated to corporate prayer. I am talking about a time where the church gathers with one mind, with one purpose and with one accord. We would see outpourings of the Holy Spirit. We would see miraculous healing. We would see people delivered from a multitude of bondages. If we would get back to this type of corporate prayer life in our church, we would see salvations like we have never had in our lifetime. In the first church this was commonplace. The last verses of Acts two describes to us the unity of the church and how they met together daily. Because of this unity in prayer and worship, the Lord added to the church daily such as would be saved. This this the key to real church growth!

One of the very first verses that I memorized as a young person in Sunday School was James 5:16. In this, James, the brother of Jesus writes, The effectual fervent prayer of a righteous man availeth much.
If we want to see results in our prayer life, then this must be the formula that we use. When we pray with purpose and when we pray in unity with our brothers and sisters in Christ and in obedience to God's will for our lives, then we will see God move and we will see the miracles that I wrote about earlier. We can read all the resources we want about prayer. We can study the books of the modern church leader. However, until we pray with that power and authority that is rightfully ours, then we will continue to pray weak and ineffective prayers. I do not want that and hopefully, neither do you. My friends, as we approach this Christmas season, let us not forsake our prayer life. May we not let the busyness of this time keep us from the appointed time of prayer. I know a vast number of believers prayed during the time leading up to the last presidential election, and we can see the results of that humbling of ourselves before God. We can not afford to stop now, we must continue to pray. In 1 Thessalonians 5:17, Paul instructs the church at Thessalonica, Pray without ceasing. This is wise instruction for us all and if we just heed that lesson, we will see remarkable things happen in our country, in our churches, in our homes and in our own lives. My goal for the church that I pastor is when things happen among our people, others can look at the blessings poured out on them and say to themselves, "and they prayed." Be blessed my friends, and do not stop praying.

A Short Treatise on the Significance of the Apocryphal Texts:
To Searchers of Truths

By Zernalyn Palmares
(Arlington, Texas)

What Are Apocryphal Texts?

The term "apocryphal" generally refers to writings that are not included in the official canon of scripture as recognized by specific religious traditions. In Christianity, this often pertains to texts that were excluded from the New Testament. The word itself comes from the Greek "apokryphos," meaning "hidden" or "secret."

Among the most well-known apocryphal texts are the Gnostic gospels, such as the Gospel of Thomas and the Gospel of Mary. These texts often present alternative narratives about Jesus and his teachings, diverging significantly from canonical accounts. Other examples include the Protoevangelium of James, which elaborates on the life of Mary and the infancy of Jesus, and the Acts of Paul and Thecla, which features a female disciple challenging societal norms.

The renewed interest in apocryphal texts today can be attributed to several key factors:

1. **Diversity of Thought**

Many people are seeking alternative spiritual paths and are drawn to the diverse perspectives offered by apocryphal texts. These writings challenge traditional narratives and provide insights into early Christianity's pluralism, catering to those who wish to explore beyond established dogmas.

2. **Historical Understanding**

Scholars and enthusiasts are increasingly interested in understanding the historical context of early Christianity. Apocryphal texts shed light on the beliefs, practices, and debates of early Christians, offering a richer, more nuanced picture of the faith's development.

3. **Feminist and Inclusive Perspectives**

Many apocryphal texts highlight the roles of women and marginalized figures in early Christian communities. Works like the Gospel of Mary emphasize women's leadership and spiritual authority, resonating with contemporary movements advocating for gender equality and inclusivity in religious contexts. The apocryphal texts were not included in the Bible as we know it today for several reasons, primarily related to theological, historical, and political factors:

1. **Canonization Process**

The process of canonization, which determined which texts were considered authoritative, was complex and varied across different Christian communities. Early church leaders debated the legitimacy and theological alignment of various writings, leading to a gradual consensus on the canon. Many apocryphal texts were deemed nonconforming to the emerging orthodoxy.

2. **Theological Discrepancies**

Many apocryphal texts contain teachings and narratives that diverge significantly from those found in the canonical gospels. For instance, Gnostic writings often emphasize secret knowledge and personal revelation, which contrast with the communal and doctrinal focus of the canonical texts. As the Church sought to define its core beliefs, texts that conflicted with these beliefs were often excluded.

3. **Authority and Authenticity**

Church leaders prioritized texts believed to be written by apostles or their close associates, as these were considered to carry authoritative teachings. Many apocryphal texts lacked clear apostolic authorship or were attributed to figures not recognized by the early church, leading to doubts about their authenticity and legitimacy.

4. **Political and Ecclesiastical Factors**

The early Church was not only a spiritual community but also a political entity. As it gained power, particularly after the Edict of Milan in 313 CE, the establishment sought to unify doctrine and practice. Texts that could potentially foster division or dissent were often suppressed or excluded to maintain cohesion.

5. **Regional Variations**

Different Christian communities had varying texts they revered. As the Church sought to create a standardized canon, texts that were popular in one region might not have been recognized in another. This regional diversity contributed to the exclusion of many apocryphal writings.

6. **Historical Context**

Many apocryphal texts were written in contexts that the early church deemed heretical or unorthodox. For example, Gnosticism was viewed as a significant threat to mainstream Christianity, prompting church leaders to reject texts associated with Gnostic beliefs.

The exclusion of apocryphal texts from the Bible reflects a complex interplay of theological, historical, and political factors. As the early Church sought to define its identity and beliefs, it made decisions that would shape the development of Christian doctrine and the formation of the biblical canon, ultimately leaving a rich tapestry of alternative writings outside the official scripture

The renewed interest in apocryphal texts reflects a broader cultural shift toward exploration, inclusivity, and personal spirituality.

For modern seekers of truth, these writings provide valuable insights and alternative narratives that enrich their understanding of faith and identity. As individuals continue to seek deeper connections with the divine, apocryphal texts will likely remain a significant resource, inviting exploration and fostering a more nuanced approach to spirituality in the contemporary landscape.

A Revolutionary Election

By Carol Milder
Chair, Republican Party, Leon County, Texas

I believe America's 2024 election was a Revolutionary election, a Declaration of Independence election, a Let Freedom Ring election, an epic historic election, a saving our country from the brink of destruction election!!

Donald Trump, like our founding fathers pledged his life, his fortune and his sacred honor. When he was shot, and miraculously stood up shouting, "FIGHT, FIGHT, FIGHT" it was a battle cry for all of us, for all patriots.

When you look at the election maps, they reveal that We The People showed up and voted, from coast to coast, from the north, south, east and west. We The People made this election TOO BIG TO RIG … we have more coverage than Verizon!!

The maps prove what most Americans know, there are no blue states, just large blue cities.

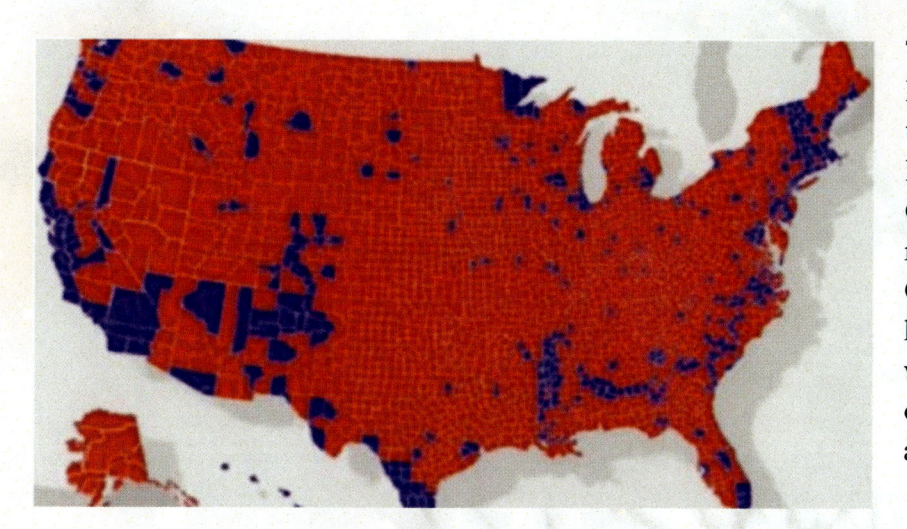

The voice of the electorate let the D.C. Bureaucrats, the Woke mob, the Progressives, the Open Boarder Liberals and those with a Global Agenda know that we are not buying what they are selling! Conservative patriots possess this land, from sea to shining sea. The voters in the rural states canceled out the votes of the large urban areas.

It was said over and over during the campaign that Republican candidates were an "Existential Threat to Democracy," but in reality, the Republican candidates are an Existential Threat to the Washington Bureaucracy.

The Bureaucrats do not tuck their tails and go home after a landslide loss, they regroup. There are plans to infiltrate rural areas, they play the long game. Patriots must stay engaged in the fight for Freedom. This election was not a finish line. There is no finish line, this side of heaven, when it comes to freedom.

My hope is that American Patriots will remain a force for Liberty, a Guardian of Liberty and Freedom. We must work together, get involved on the local level, stay informed and fight the good fight for freedom, together.

Fight, Fight, Fight!! Pray, Pray, Pray!!

2 Chronicles 7:14- *"If my people, who are called by my name, shall humble themselves, and pray, and seek my face, and turn from their wicked ways; then will I hear from heaven, and will forgive their sin, and will heal their land"*

Carol Milder is the County Chair for the Republican Party of Leon County, Texas. She has been a dynamic force to galvanize the Republican influence in the east Texas area. Carol has been a resident of Leon County for many years, and has recently retired from her long held, well-respected real estate appraisal company, working all areas in an eastern swath that extended from south of Dallas to south of Houston. She has faithfully represented the values and concerns of the "down home" conservative American population of that area and beyond. We are happy to have her contribution this month to Christian Times Magazine.

The True Meaning of Christmas

By Charles Lingerfelt

(Luke 2:10,11)

When we gather this Christmas season, we will be reminded of the most extraordinary event in the history of mankind —the birth of Jesus Christ.

While it's so easy to get lost in the festivities of the season, the lights, and the gifts, we must remember at its core, Christmas is a celebration of something much deeper. It is the celebration of God's greatest gift to the world—a gift that transcends time and space. It is the gift of hope, love, and new beginnings. The true meaning of Christmas is not just about the story of a baby born in a manger—it's about the transformation that His birth brings to our lives.

"But the angel said to them, "Do not be afraid. I bring you good news that will cause great joy for all the people. 11 Today in the town of David a Savior has been born to you; he is the Messiah, the Lord." (Luke 2:10-11) NIV

This announcement, made to the lowly shepherds on that holy night, was not just for a select few—it was for the whole world. The birth of Jesus was the answer to humanity's deepest longing, the fulfillment of God's promise to bring peace, joy, and salvation to all who would receive Him.

The Meaning of Christmas:

1. It is Hope for the Hopeless -
Christmas speaks to our deepest need for hope. In a world often filled with despair, Christmas reminds us that God did not leave us in our brokenness. He sent His Son to bring light into our darkness, to bring hope to our hopelessness.

The angel's announcement of Jesus' birth was not just good news for the shepherds—it was good news for the entire world, for every man, woman, and child who has ever lived. Jesus came to restore what was lost, to heal what was broken, and to bring us hope beyond our circumstances.

There is a story about a man named Alex who was searching for something he couldn't put into words. Growing up in a tough neighborhood, Alex struggled with a sense of worthlessness. He had made poor decisions that had cost him friendships, family, and hope. One cold Christmas Eve, feeling utterly alone, he wandered into a church service. The pastor spoke about the birth of Jesus, not just as a historical event, but as a promise of hope for everyone, especially those who felt forgotten.

That night, Alex felt a spark in his heart—a hope he had never known. For the first time, he understood that Jesus came for people like him, people who felt lost and unworthy. That Christmas, Alex gave his life to Christ, and he began to see a future filled with possibility.

We need to remember that the gift of Christmas is a message of hope for the hopeless.

No matter where we are in life, no matter how deep our struggles, Jesus offers us the hope of a new tomorrow.

2. It is Love That Transcends Everything -

At the heart of Christmas is love—a love that does not depend on our performance, our appearance, or our past. It is a love that is unconditional, unshakeable, and eternal.

The Bible tells us that "God is love" (1 John 4:8). And the birth of Jesus is the clearest demonstration of this love. God loved us so much that He sent His Son to be "with us," to live among us, to walk in our shoes. Jesus' coming was not just a gift—it was an invitation to experience the depth of God's love, a love that knows no boundaries.

3. The True Meaning of Christmas is Great Joy -

In the beginning, the God of joy made a world of joys — a creation full of good, altogether "very good," and primed to delight in His creatures (Genesis 1:31; 2:9). As the work of His hands, we know joy. We have tasted His goodness in His world, even on this side of sin's curse. We have experienced, however meagerly or infrequently, the blessed emotional surges of God-made delight — in a kind word, in a friend's hug, in our team's victory, in a cool breeze, in good food and drink. We know normal joy and we know what it is.

But Christmas is not normal joy. Christmas, the Gospels say, is great joy. Christmas is not natural joy, but supernatural. God set Christmas apart. He himself has come down in the person of His Son.

The Word has become flesh. The long-awaited Savior is born. When the angel heralds his arrival, he says, "I bring you good news of great joy" (Luke 2:10). And when pagan astrologers traversed from afar and find him, "they rejoiced exceedingly with great joy" (Matthew 2:10).

God gave to us a world of joys to prompt our readiness for this miraculous moment in our lives when an Angel would announce "great joy" for all people; a time when just simple joy would no longer be enough. God gave us joy for Christmas joy to surpass it. And that must always be remembered by us about Christmas!

Therefore, let us Celebrate with Hope, with Love, and with Great Joy the miraculous and wonderful Savior and Messiah: Jesus the Christ and Lord over all.

Merry Christmas to Everyone!

Lovingly yours,

Charles Lingerfelt,
Editor-In-Chief

CHRISTIAN LEARNING CENTER
RELEASED TIME BIBLE EDUCATION

CAMPBELL COUNTY
CHRISTIAN LEARNING CENTER

Lighting the path to Release Time Bible Education for public school students Promoting and protecting parents' rights in education

The Campbell County Christian Learning Center (CCCLC) exists to provide biblical instruction to students as an opportunity to encourage them to embrace the Gospel of Jesus Christ, grow in the Christian faith, and apply biblical principles for living

> "ALL SCRIPTURE IS INSPIRED BY GOD AND IS PROFITABLE FOR TEACHING, FOR REBUKING, FOR CORRECTING, FOR TRAINING IN RIGHTEOUSNESS, SO THAT THE MAN OF GOD MAY BE COMPLETE, EQUIPPED FOR EVERY GOOD WORK."
> 2 TIMOTHY 3:16-17

Phone: 423-377-5696

CONTACT US:

Mailing: PO Box 256, Lafollette, Tennessee 37766
Email: campbellCLC2018@gmail.com | Website: www.campbellcountyclc.org

CCCLC is a 501(C) charitable organization funded solely by private donations

This Advertisement Paid For By A Concerned Christian Believer!

Merry Christmas AND HAPPY NEW YEAR

Sid Miller
Texas Agriculture Commissioner

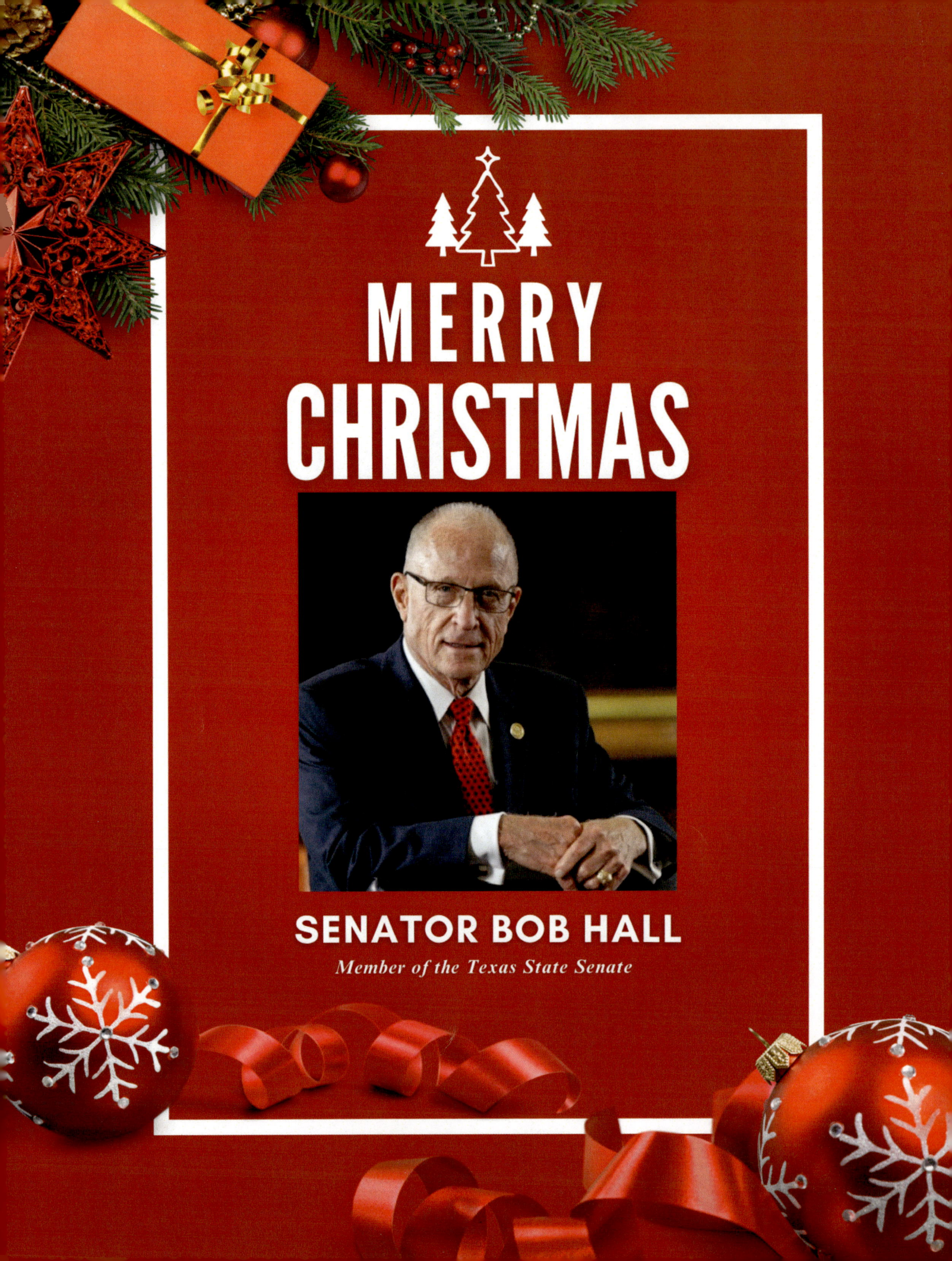

MERRY CHRISTMAS

SENATOR BOB HALL

Member of the Texas State Senate

THUNDER IN THE MOUNTAINS

AUTHOR:
MICKEY NICHOLS

AVAILABLE ON

amazon

BARNES & NOBLE

Merry Christmas Mr. President

Keep Christ in Christmas

Let's celebrate the birth of Jesus with joy and thanksgiving. Wishing you a blessed Christmas.

Merry Christmas to All

From

Potter County GOP
PotterCountyGOP.com

Become Informed Included and Invested

We The People Townsquare
WeThePeopleTownSquare.com

Start your own *Operation Show*: Attend Local meetings from School Boards to City Council.

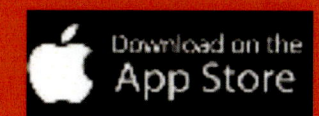

Join us at

WeThePeopleTownsquare.com

God's love is all around us this Christmas! Wishing you and yours, joy and happiness.

Help us restore Honor to our Republic

MORE THAN JUST A GUARD COMPANY
WE PROVIDE UNIQUE SECURITY SOLUTIONS TO THE GREAT STATE OF TEXAS

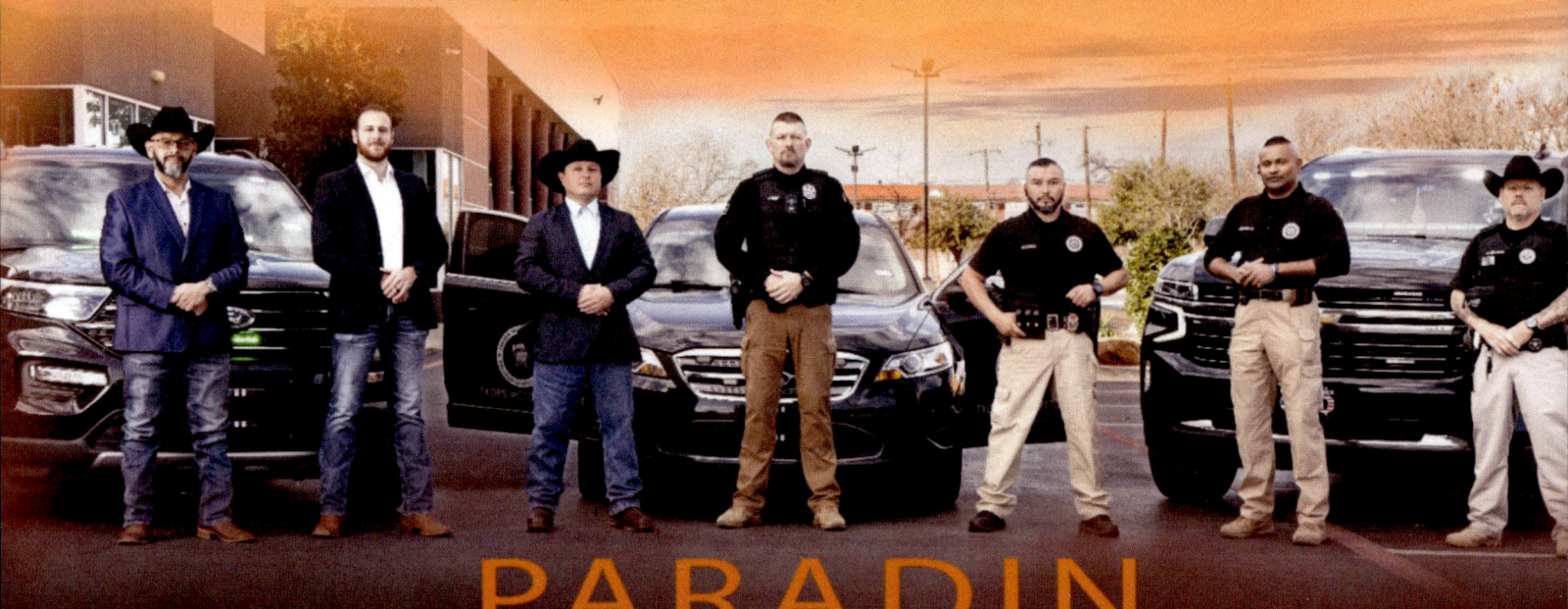

PARADIN
SECURITY SOLUTIONS LLC
TXDPS# C10591701

STRATEGIC SECURITY SOLUTIONS. LEGITIMATE SECURITY PROFESSIONALS. STRATEGIC SAFETY CONSULTING. LICENSES AND CERTIFICATIONS. QUALITY ASSETS. INFORMATION ACQUISITION.

PH: 469-383-0311/469-650-7123 EMAIL: J.KURUVILLA@PARADINSECURITY.COM/R.LINGERFELT@PARADINSECURITY.COM

WWW.PARADINSECURITY.COM

Contact:

Johnson Kuruvilla: 469.383.0311

Ryan Lingerfelt: 469.650.7123

PARADIN
www.paradinsecurity.com

MERRY *Christmas*

AND HAPPY NEW YEAR

SEN. TED CRUZ

JOURNEY INTO FAITH AND PATRIOTISM

AVAILABLE ON

AMAZON & BARNES & NOBLE